The Dirty Mom's Playbook;
How To Win Custody Like A

A BULLET PROOF PLAN TO WIN PRIMARY CUSTODY.

INCLUDES: JOURNAL, WORKSHEETS, AND CHECKLISTS TO WIN THE FIGHT OF YOUR LIFE.

A RECENT NEWS ITEM SHOWED A MOTHER ATTACKING A MOUNTAIN LION WHO SNATCHED HER CHILD. THE MOTHER MENTIONED WAS NOT ALIENATING HER CHILD FROM THE MOUNTAIN LION. THE MOTHER'S ONLY CONCERN, LIKE MOST MOTHERS IN CONTESTED CUSTODY CASES IS TO PROTECT HER CHILDREN. COURT PROFESSIONALS WITHOUT THE NECESSARY DOMESTIC VIOLENCE KNOWLEDGE TEND TO FOCUS ON THE MYTH THAT MOTHERS FREQUENTLY MAKE FALSE REPORTS AND ASSUME THEY ARE ACTING OUT OF VINDICTIVENESS. MOTHERS FACING COURTS WITH THESE COMMON AND FALSE BELIEFS DO NOT RECEIVE FAIR TRIALS.

TAKEN FROM THE NOMAS WEBSITE

THIS JOURNAL IS CO-WRITTEN BY A SINGLE MOTHER WHO HAS SURVIVED NARCISSISTIC ABUSE AND HER OWN MOTHER, WHO HAS BEEN HAPPILY MARRIED FOR 50 YEARS AND IS A TOP THERAPIST SPECIALIZING IN RELATIONSHIPS AND PERSONALITY DISORDERS. DESPITE THEIR DIFFERENT LIVES, THEY'VE COME TOGETHER TO CREATE A PLAN FOR ABUSE VICTIMS THAT CUTS THROUGH THE BULLSHIT.

NARCISSISTS AND OTHER TOXIC PEOPLE WITH PERSONALITY DISORDERS ARE MORE COMMON AND DANGEROUS THAN WE REALIZE, CAUSING WIDESPREAD DEVASTATION THAT SOCIETY IS UNPREPARED FOR. PEOPLE OFTEN BELIEVE THIS ISSUE ONLY AFFECTS THOSE WITH LOW INCOMES OR ABUSIVE BACKGROUNDS, ASSUMING EDUCATED INDIVIDUALS WOULD NEVER FALL PREY TO NARCISSISTS. THIS COULDN'T BE FURTHER FROM THE TRUTH.

MEGGAN AND HER MOM LINDA HAVE A CRUCIAL MESSAGE, BUT MORE IMPORTANTLY, THEY OFFER A PRACTICAL PLAN FOR ANYONE TRAPPED WITH OR SUSPECTING A LOVED ONE HAS A PERSONALITY DISORDER.

THEY'VE CREATED A POWERFUL GUIDE FOR DEFEATING NARCISSISTS AND TAKING BACK CONTROL OF YOUR LIFE. THEIR PRIMARY FOCUS IS ON THE CHILDREN INVOLVED AND THE CRITICAL IMPORTANCE OF PROTECTING THEM FROM A NARCISSISTIC PARENT.

This journal didn't find you by accident. You're holding it because it's meant for you. I poured my heart and soul into this for you.

I know right now it feels like your world is falling apart, and no one around you truly understands what you're going through,

and you're right, most people have no idea.

But some of us have walked in your shoes, and we've come out victorious.

Right now, I'm here with you, every step of the way. That won't change, because I'm going to walk with you through the end..

Use this journal to help you believe in yourself as a woman and a mother. Your love for your children can move mountains, but the lies and manipulation of a narcissist can move even bigger ones.

That's why you need a plan, and that plan has to be driven by your love for your children.

A mother's love is chaotic, intense, emotional, and beautiful. Most importantly, it's powerful beyond words. So powerful, that it's indescribable.

So, turning that love into a strategic plan for battle can feel overwhelming and frankly it sounds "impossible AF."

But don't worry, you're not alone.

You will win custody of your kids because you are their mother, and no one can take that away from you.

No judge, lawyer, or social worker will dictate when you can see your children. No ex will get more time with your kids, regardless of how good a father he is. He didn't carry them, birth them from his vagina, or nourish them from his tits. That's your role, given to you by God. If your ex was meant to raise your kids full time, God would have made him a mother.

But he didn't. God made you a mother.

And no one's going to take that from you.

Your narcissistic ex won't strip away your purpose because he lacks the courage to be a real man.

So, turn the page and give this everything you've got.

If protecting and loving your children is your life's mission, then you've already succeeded. There's no greater achievement than being a mother.

So, fight hard, because if you *don't* win, your gonna die trying.

Meggan Jean

Date:__________

Today is the start of my new beginning.

A PROMISE TO MYSELF:

Today, I will put the fear of him behind me. I will no longer live my life out of fear for what he may or may not do.

Remember:

Nothing he can ever say or do, can make me someone I'm not.

I was chosen to be a mother.
It wasnt an accident or a coincidence.

Envision Your Victory:

- Reflect on the significance of the quote from Jeremiah 1:5.

How does the idea of being chosen to be a mother resonate with you?

Take some time to journal your thoughts and feelings about your journey to motherhood.

- List the names of your children and take a moment to reflect on each one.

As you do this, think about the unique qualities and characteristics that make them special to you.

- Consider whether you believe that each of your children were intentionally placed in your life for a purpose.

How does this belief influence your perspective on parenthood and your role as a mother?

You will teach them to fly, but they will not fly your flight. You will teach them to dream, but they will not dream your dream. You will teach them to live, but they will not live your life. Nevertheless, in every flight, in every life, in every dream, the print of the way you taught them will remain."
-Mother Teresa

- Think about the challenges you've faced in your journey as a parent, especially in navigating custody battles with a narcissistic partner.

How does your faith or sense of purpose help you find strength and resilience during difficult times?

- Reflect on your journey through the challenges and hardships you've faced in your efforts to protect and care for your children.

If given the choice, would you go through it all again for the sake of your children?

Consider the sacrifices you've made and the strength you've discovered within yourself. Journal your thoughts and feelings about the profound love and resilience that drives you to persevere, even in the face of adversity.

Narcissists will typically be playing offense against you, especially when you leave them. This is when they start their infamous smear campaign.

So what do you do?
If you do nothing, everyday you'll be defending yourself against a new allegation.
That is no way to live.

Ill never forget when I was in the middle of my custody battle, and every day I was waking up to a new horrible allegation that would litterally drain my soul. If it wasn't a DHS report, it was a restraining order, or a report to my employer.
My ex was an extreme case, but no one should have to deal with any type of false allegations.
My therapist told me that narcissists do this because theyre trying to punish their ex for leaving. Their goal is to teach a lesson, so their ex will decide that it's easier just to go back to them.
This thought crossed my mind a lot.
"Maybe I should just go back, maybe I can't do this."
One day, a friend told me that I needed to start focusing on playing the offense, so then my ex would be the one defending himself, and he wouldn't have the time to sit and focus on what he could do to hurt me. This seemed like it made perfect sense at the time, but it was not the right move to make.

—Meg

So should you focus on offense or defense?

Neither.
You should hide the ball
because without a ball
there can be
no game to play.

Now what do I mean by this?

This means that you already know your ex isn't going to play fair, whether you focus on offense or your defense.

SO TAKE AWAY HIS ABILITY TO PLAY.

This will piss your narcissist off,
because narcs can't handle
having things taken away from them.
When that happens, they act like newborn ninnies
who pout, throw tantrums,
piss their pants, etc.

They just do a "gifted" or "big boy" version of this. Examples are: giving you the silent treatment, not allowing you to talk with the kids on the phone during his time, or being an hour late to bring the kids home.

Examples of balls:

1. Your real phone number.
2. Any passwords he may have to your social media accounts.
3. Time alone with you that is unwitnessed or unrecorded.
4. Bank account information.
5. Your home address or any details about your living situation.
6. Details about your work schedule or place of employment.
7. Information about your children's schools and activities.
8. Access to your medical records or personal health information.
9. Communication with mutual friends who might share your information.
10. Any plans you have regarding vacations or travel.

BY LIMITING HIS ACCESS TO THESE ASPECTS OF YOUR LIFE, YOU MINIMIZE HIS ABILITY TO CREATE CHAOS AND MAKE FALSE ALLEGATIONS. IT'S ABOUT TAKING CONTROL AND ENSURING HE DOESN'T HAVE THE AMMUNITION TO CONTINUE HIS SMEAR CAMPAIGN. FOCUS ON PROTECTING YOUR INFORMATION AND MAINTAINING YOUR PRIVACY, SO YOU CAN LIVE YOUR LIFE WITHOUT CONSTANT FEAR OF THE NEXT ATTACK.

Here are three examples of things that my ex did to me that could have been prevented, had I just hidden the balls:

<u>Turned in false text messages</u>:

Because he had my phone number, he was able to download a text-now app, and make it appear as though I had sent him horrible text messages where I appeared to have threatened him, threatened my children, or where I was admitting to using drugs. Now this seems unreal, but my ex did this. He actually did it several different times, and he used them to get restraining orders, to make DHS reports, and for leverage in our custody. It didn't matter that I could show the judge my legal time-stamped logs, showing I never sent any such messages. Every Judge still allowed my exes fake messages in as evidence and gave them "the weight they thought they deserved." I don't believe that judges have the training, or the time to try and decipher what time-stamped logs even are. I also believe that in general, it's hard for anyone to really accept that someone would go to such extremes and lie about things like this. Remember, your ex plays the victim so well, that most people will want to believe him. This is extremely serious because you could be accused of anything, and could potentially end up in jail before ever getting a chance to fight it. The scariest thing, is that your ex doesn't even need an app to make it look like you sent him a text message. My attorney figured out exactly what he was doing, and anyone can make it look like someone texted their phone just by using a simple trick. Had I changed my phone number, and only communicated with him through a parenting app, or third party....he wouldn't have been able to come up with these messages.

Many people don't realize that anyone can go into any courthouse, and ask for a No Contact Order. All that is required to get a judge to sign one, is saying that you feel threatened. One can feel threatened by another person because someone physically hurt you, or just because someone *threatened* to hurt you. A judge has to error on the side of caution and issue a temporary No Contact Order if he/she feels the victim may be in danger. Then they set a hearing in the next 10-15 days. Possibly longer if one party asks for a continuance. A person can also add their minor children to the NCO, if it's one of their parents who are dangerous.

So once the judge signs off, the sherrif goes and serves the person who is considered dangerous, and they cannot go within 300 feet of the victim or the children until the court date. Now this is great for people who truly need protection. But what happens when someone like your ex goes and asks for one against you? Is it fair that you have to wait 15 days to go tell a judge that your in fact the victim? Oh, and I forgot to mention, when the sheriff comes to your home to serve you, or the "dangerous person", they will take the children as well without any warning, and give them to the "victim"

My ex did this a few times, and the main goal for him was to take my twin daughters from me. Once I left him, he knew that the only way to hurt me was to take my daughters from me. Even if he knew that in 15 days, I would get them back, it was worth the pain he got to cause me to have no contact with them. The sickest part is that these situations cause serious trauma on children. They have no idea why they're suddenly not able to see their mother, but the narcissist doesn't care about that. He cares more about hurting you, and punishing you for leaving, then he cares for his own children.

On this example I'm about to share with you, I had finally really started to set and stick to my boundaries, and my ex couldn't handle it.

He had kept my daughters for a weekend visit before labor day, and on the sunday he was supposed to return them to my home where he knew my parents would be witnesses at, he baited me to come get them at a local park. He argued with me the whole day, threatening to not bring the girls home at all. The last part of the day he just stopped responding to me completely, so I was worried and jumped at any chance just to get them home. He finally gave me an option to come pick them up at the park, otherwise he threatened to just keep them for the week. Of course, I headed for the park. It was a mistake I've lived to regret. He used this specific interaction with me for several different false allegations, but the first one was 2 weeks after the incident. He got a restraining order, saying in a 4- page letter to the judge, that I physically assaulted him at the park. Had I not let down my guard and stuck to my boundaries of having a witness at all exchanges, he would have never had this one interaction with me to use to his advantage. Now again, your ex could go tell a judge that you assaulted him whether your alone with him or not, but it's a lot less likely if you truly aren't around him alone.

<u>Ruined Family Vacations:</u>

Like always, I gave my ex the benefit of the doubt and continued to believe that I could co-parent with him. I was trying to follow our temporary custody stipulation, and informed my ex that I would be taking the kids to the waterpark in Minnesota on an upcoming weekend. Before we left, he asked if he could come up with us and stay with us to watch the girls experience the park. When I denied his request, he flipped out over text message and said that he never gave me permission to take the girls out of state. The entire trip to the waterpark my was stressful for me because he was sending me text after text. When I arrived at the hotel, it was storming outside, I had both sets of my twins, along with my daughters friend, so I had 5 kids under the age of 8. It was late by the time we arrived and the kids were starving and were dying to go swimming before the park closed. When I tried checking in, the hotel clerk informed me that my reservation had been cancelled earlier that day by a male who called and said we weren't coming. They had given my hotel room away and were completely booked. I had saved my money for that trip, and they had refunded my debit card but it would take up to 30 days for it to be back on my card. So there i was with 5 hungry kids, in a big city with no money in the middle of a storm. We were thankfully comped a presidential suite by the manager for the mistake of cancelling it....but my ex threatened me with the police and welfare checks all weekend, and of course he got away with this. Now I am all for following court orders because one thing you don't want to look like to a judge, is someone who isn't following a court order. You want to be the parent who is trying to cooperate. BUT, there are some rules your going to need to break, or get around for your own safety and sanity. You have to get creative. Had I not told my ex the truth about where we were going, or just altered the truth a little, he wouldnt have been able to ruin my trip with my children. Remember, this is the Dirty Mom's Playbook. Sometimes with a narcissist, you have to get dirty to beat them at their own game. Ill explain more about that later.

<u>Reflection Exercise:</u>

<u>List the false allegations or harmful actions your ex has taken against you.</u>
As you write each one, reflect in your mind how these actions have impacted your life and what steps you can take to prevent them from happening again.

If your ex has not made any false allegations against you, list possible allegations that you could see him making against you. You wouldn't have this journal if you didn't have a toxic ex. Remember, Toxic people will go to extremes to hurt others, including making false allegations.

Lastly, imagine that the whole world believed each allegation, including your custody judge. Was the allegation serious enough to possibly effect you losing custody of your children? If so, the level of danger your ex puts you in goes way up. Some plans may need to be adjusted depending on how dangerous your ex is. More on that later..

- ~~**False Allegations.**~~   **Serious?**

☐	Y/N
☐	Y/N
☐	Y/N
☐	Y/N
☐	Y/N
☐	Y/N

False Allegations. Serious?
Y/N
Y/N
Y/N
Y/N
Y/N
Y/N

Prevention Strategies

In the space below, write down practical steps you can take to prevent false allegations by your ex in the future. Consider measures to protect your privacy, secure your information, and build a strong support network.

Prevention Strategies Checklist

Personal Information:

Change your phone number and share it only with trusted individuals.

Update all passwords for social media, email, and other online accounts.

Secure your bank account information and ensure only you have access.

Communication:

Avoid any unwitnessed or unrecorded time alone with your ex.

Document all interactions with your ex (texts, emails, phone calls) and keep them organized. *See page 27 for more information about documentation.*

Only communicate through a parenting app. If he won't agree, then only communicate through a third party. *See page 27. The parenting app CANNOT BE STRESSED ENOUGH! This changed my entire situation around, and in the end sealed my custody case in my favor.*

Prevention Strategies Checklist Cont.

Communication cont:

- Use a separate email address for communication related to legal and custody matters.

- Install a call recording app on your phone for documenting phone conversations.

- Set up a system for documenting and timestamping all written and verbal communications.

- Consult with a lawyer to understand your rights and legal options.

- Keep important legal documents (custody agreements, restraining orders) in a safe place.

- Notify relevant authorities (e.g., police, employer) about your situation and any existing restraining orders. File police reports or legal complaints for any harassment or false allegations to create an official record. *This is very important but it needs to be done very carefully. Will go into detail in phase 2 of the playbook.*

Prevention Strategies Checklist Cont.

- [ ] Create a record of any false allegations made against you, including dates, details, and any evidence that disproves them.

Support System:

- [ ] Inform trusted friends, family, and professionals about your situation and any false allegations.

- [ ] Seek therapy or counseling for emotional support and guidance. *Finding a therapist for you and your children is one of the most important things you need to do*

- [ ] Join a support group for individuals going through similar situations.

- [ ] Establish a code word with trusted friends or family for emergencies.

- [ ] Maintain regular contact with your support network to ensure you have witnesses who can vouch for your character and whereabouts.

Prevention Strategies Checklist Cont.

Support System Cont.

- Keep your home address confidential. Consider using a P.O. box for mail.

- Inform your employer about your situation and request they do not share your work schedule.

- Ensure your children's school and activities information are kept private.

- Install security cameras around your home for added protection.

- Change the locks on your home if your ex had access to keys.

- **<u>Children's Safety:</u>**
  Teach your children about personal safety and what to do if they feel unsafe.

Prevention Strategies Checklist Cont.

Child Safety Cont.

☐ Ensure your children know who they can go to for help at school or during activities.

☐ Keep a record of your children's schedules and routines for consistency and security.

☐ Monitor your children's online activity and set up parental controls if necessary.

☐ Communicate with your children's teachers and caregivers about any concerns or special instructions.

Digital Security:
☐ Use strong, unique passwords for all online accounts and change them regularly.

☐ Install antivirus and anti-malware software on all your devices.

Prevention Strategies Checklist Cont.

Digital Security Cont

- [ ] Be cautious about sharing personal information online or on social media.

- [ ] Regularly check the privacy settings on your social media accounts.

- [ ] Consider using a virtual private network (VPN) for added online privacy.

- [ ] Back up all important digital communications and documents to a secure location.

Documentation:

- [ ] Keep a detailed journal of all interactions with your ex, noting dates, times, and specifics.

- [ ] Store copies of all court orders, custody agreements, and legal communications in a safe place.

Prevention Strategies Checklist Cont.

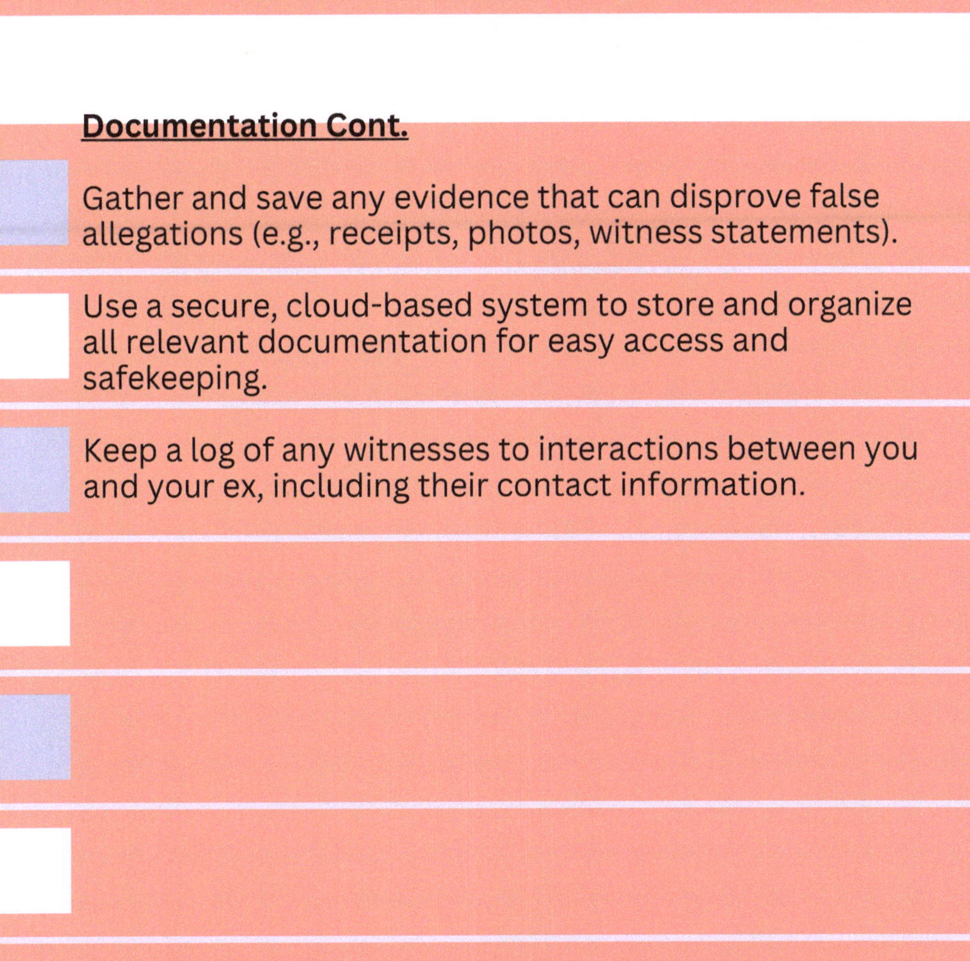

Documentation Cont.

- [ ] Gather and save any evidence that can disprove false allegations (e.g., receipts, photos, witness statements).

- [ ] Use a secure, cloud-based system to store and organize all relevant documentation for easy access and safekeeping.

- [ ] Keep a log of any witnesses to interactions between you and your ex, including their contact information.

- [ ]

- [ ]

- [ ]

Lets go over the documentation:

Document all interactions with your ex (texts, emails, phone calls) and keep them organized.

Okay, nope.

Like the last thing anyone going through a custody battle needs to hear is *"document everything."*

Like wow, really? I've never heard that genius idea.

Obviously, we need to remember the important interactions that could prove to any moron your ex is fucking crazy, but if you truly have a narcissistic ex, every single interaction with them will become something that should be documented.

Every conversation makes your jaw drop, so honestly it seems impossible to "document" everything, especially when your consumed with trying to defend yourself against his make -believe stories, all while still being a good mom to your kids, without letting them know that your shits falling apart because their dad is an asshole.

However, organized documentation is <u>crucial</u>. So, what's the solution?

There are three parts to documenting for custody. But the first step is getting a parenting app and using it for all communication. These apps allow you to export text messages into a PDF with a single click, making it easy to print, store, or save on your computer. This way you won't have to piece together old texts and call logs, and the parenting app chats cannot be edited or altered, so this prevents your ex from denying he sent you such abusive messages. Everything is documented in one place.

You've just completed the end of Dirty Mom's Playbook - Phase 1

This was meant to be an exploration of what your situation is, and in the following phases, we break down exactly what we will do to win custody.

WE HOPE YOU'LL CONTINUE ALLOWING US TO WALK WITH YOU ON YOUR JOURNEY, AND WE'LL SEE YOU IN PHASE 2 OF OUR CUSTODY JOURNAL.

PHASE 2: You'll learn why Great Documentation is the **number one** reason a parent wins custody of their children.
It's also the **number one** struggle that parents in custody battles say they don't understand how to do.

If your wanting extra support, we've created simple, easy to understand worksheets that you can use over and over again. Our newest worksheet is specifically geared to help you document for your custody case, or for anything you might need to have documentation for.

Proper documentation is the beginning step to stop your ex from ruining your life.

Remember, it's never too early to start documenting, and it's never too late to begin.

THIS JOURNAL
BELONGS TO:

____

____

____

NOTES:

NOTES: